Gold Boxes

The
Wrightsman
Collection GOLD
BOXES

Text by CLARE LE CORBEILLER

Photographs by MALCOLM VARON

The Metropolitan Museum of Art

Copyright © 1977 by The Metropolitan Museum of Art

LIBRARY OF CONGRESS CATALOGING IN PUBLICATION DATA

New York (City). Metropolitan Museum of Art.
  Gold boxes.

  Catalog of a permanent exhibit at the Metropolitan Museum
of Art, New York.
  1. Gold boxes—New York (City)—Catalogs. 2. Goldwork,
Rococo—New York (City)—Catalogs. 3. Wrightsman, Charles
B.—Art collections. 4. New York (City). Metropolitan Museum
of Art. I. Le Corbeiller, Clare. II. Varon, Malcolm. III. Title.

NK7102.N4N476 1977   739.2′274′07401471   77-23592
ISBN 0-87099-166-3

An object of use, luxury, and superb craftsmanship: the gold box in the eighteenth century was all of these. It was by definition a snuff box, although it often held jewels, money, or even a scroll conferring the freedom of a city. Conventionally it was oblong, circular, or oval, but the Duchess of Orléans owned a gondola-shaped snuff box and Madame de Pompadour one in the form of a cat. Some boxes were made entirely of gold—polished, matted, chased, engraved, and even tinted. On others, the gold was set off by enameling. Figures or still lifes in bright opaque colors were painted directly onto the gold surface (*en plein*), trails of vines and flowers were carved out of the surface, the spaces filled with shimmering translucent shades of blue and green (*basse taille*). Other boxes were little more than gold frames fitted with panels of another material: hardstones, porcelain, lacquer, mother-of-pearl, and miniature paintings were all used in their design.

The snuff box was an eighteenth-century phenomenon, the counterpart for its time of the pendant jewels of the Renaissance and the Easter eggs and jeweled accessories by Fabergé in the nineteenth century. It came into being in the early 1700s when snuff-taking became socially acceptable. It began to go out of favor about a hundred years later. During that century the Parisian goldsmiths and retail merchants (*marchands merciers*) set a standard of craftsmanship and imagination that prevailed throughout western Europe. Because the snuff box was essentially an element of costume, its style changed as often as fashions do, and commissions from the French court and nobility alone insured a steady, demanding market for the newest designs.

Most of these changes in taste are reflected in the boxes of the Wrightsman Collection. The earliest in the group were made in the 1730s, the decade in which the gold box came of age, and display the vigorous asymmetrical scrollwork of the early rococo style (1, 2). Typical of the 1740s are two boxes of plain shape covered with a sinuous unbroken pattern (4, 5). The range of enameling techniques and effects is demonstrated by a number of boxes that include one by Jean Frémin patterned with high-relief flower sprays (13), another by Noël Hardivillers smoothly painted with still-life compositions (9), an example of Charles Le Bastier's modern use of contrasting colors and textures (20), and a German box attributed to Daniel Baudesson, its detailed allegorical subjects enameled with perfect control (8).

The *tabatière à cage* epitomizes the gold box as an object *à la mode*: the owner had only to change the panels in his box to keep up to date without incurring a new expense for the gold. The *tabatière à cage* also enabled the *marchands merciers* (who are credited with at least popularizing, if not inventing, it) to purchase frames from goldsmiths and assemble the boxes themselves, using materials it was their prerogative to market, such as porcelain and lacquer. A box by Jean Ducrollay with panels of shell and lacquer (16) would have been produced in this way, and it was undoubtedly a *marchand mercier* who took a gold frame made in 1748/9 and refitted it in 1767 with miniature views of the château of Chanteloup (15). A variant of this practice is believed to account for the present appearance of another box by Ducrollay, decorated with portrait miniatures of members of the French royal family (14). Not a *tabatière à cage,* this box was probably originally studded with oval pieces of agate or other hardstone.

In general, the role of the goldsmith in the design of these mixed-media boxes was limited to the execution of decorative panels and borders. It was in boxes carried out entirely in gold that the goldsmith and chaser (*ciseleur*) had free rein and could bring into play a greater repertoire of techniques. On an early box by Ducrollay (1) an effect of distant landscapes, chased in low relief with matte surfaces, is reinforced by the large scale of their sweeping polished frames. On two other boxes, one English (3), one French (18), the art of the *ciseleur* is seen at its most developed. Exceptionally, the chasing on each box is signed. For the most part, the artists who contributed to the decoration of gold boxes are anonymous, and a box is traditionally said to have been made by the master goldsmith whose mark is struck on it. The signatures of Gérard Debèche and George Michael Moser remind us of the specialization inherent in the manufacture of a gold box; further, they invite us to enjoy in the finished work the sense of individual and collaborative artistry that defines the gold box of the eighteenth century.

The Boxes

I. Jean Ducrollay *(working 1734–64/5). Paris, 1732–38*

2 . Daniel Gouers *(or Govaers, working 1717–c. 36)*,

the miniature after a painting by Rosalba Carriera (1675–1758).
Paris, 1732–36

3. P.R.,

the chasing by George Michael Moser (1704–83). London, 1741

Commissioned in 1740 for presentation to Admiral Edward Vernon (1689–1757), the box was intended to contain a scroll conferring the Freedom of the City of London on Vernon, who had captured the Caribbean city of Porto Bello from Spain the previous year.

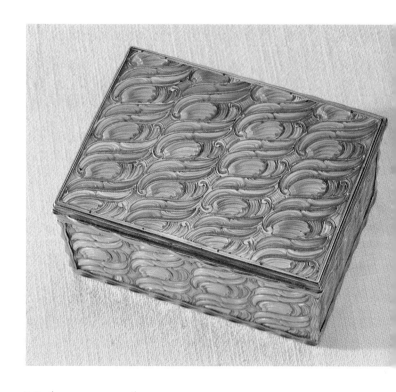

4. Unknown maker *(mark illegible)*. Paris, *1744/5*

5. Unknown maker *(no mark)*. Paris, *1748/9*

6. Unknown maker *(no mark). Paris, 1750–56*

The same imagination and skill that went into the design of gold boxes informs such other luxurious accessories as shuttles, knife handles, patch boxes, and even—as here—a case to hold two pairs of spectacles.

7. Claude Lisonnet *(working 1736–61). Paris, 1750/1*

8. Attributed to Daniel Baudesson *(working 1730–80)*, the enameling possibly by Daniel Nicolas Chodowiecki (1726–1801). Berlin, 1750–55

Baudesson worked in Berlin at the court of Frederick the Great, whose own collection of snuff boxes was extravagant both in size and taste. Although neither marked nor signed, this box has all the features of others inscribed with the names of Baudesson and Chodowiecki.

9. Noël Hardivillers *(working 1729–79). Paris, 1754/5*

10. Jean Formey *(working 1754–c. 91). Paris, 1757/8*

I I . Noël Hardivillers. *Paris, 1753/4*

12 . Barnabé Sageret *(working 1731–58),*
the miniatures by Mlle. Duplessis. Paris, 1757/8

13. Jean Frémin *(working 1738–86). Paris, 1756/7*

14. Jean Ducrollay. *Paris, 1749/50*

Each miniature on this double box depicts a member of the French royal family. Portraits of Louis XV and Marie Leszczynska are inside the two lids. On the outside are their children: "Mesdames," the five unmarried daughters; the Dauphin, the Duchess of Parma, and their families.

15. Possibly Pierre François Delafons *(working 1732–87),*

the miniatures by Louis Nicolas van Blarenberghe (1719–94).
Paris, 1748/9 and 1767

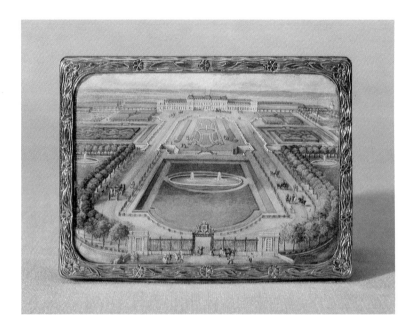

The château of Chanteloup, near Amboise, was acquired in
1761 by the Duc de Choiseul while he was Louis XV's minister
of foreign affairs. His extensive alterations to the gardens and
park are shown in van Blarenberghe's characteristically detailed
views.

17. Louis Roucel (working 1763–87). Paris, 1768/9

Dürer's print of a rhinoceros, popular from the moment it was issued in 1515, appears here on a black shell ground inlaid (*piqué*) with hair-thin strips of gold and silver that simulate the lines of the original woodcut.

18. Henry Bodson (working 1763–c. 89),

the chasing by Gérard Debèche (1706–77?). Paris, 1768/9

Engravings after François Boucher were frequently adapted by
the decorators of gold boxes. Debèche's vigorously modeled treat-
ment of Boucher compositions is in dramatic contrast to such
placid enameled versions as those on the box by Hardivillers (9).

19. Louis Charonnat *(working 1748–c. 82). Paris, 1763/4*

20. Charles Le Bastier *(working 1754–c. 83).*

   Paris, 1771/2